I Won't Go With Strangers

Written and illustrated by
Dagmar Geisler

Sky Pony Press
New York

10 9

Manufactured in China, May 2023
This product conforms to CPSIA 2008

Library of Congress Cataloging-in-Publication Data is available on file.

Cover design by Kate Gartner
Cover illustration by Dagmar Geisler

Print ISBN: 978-1-5107-3534-7
Ebook ISBN: 978-1-5107-3536-1

Lu's list:

People who are allowed to pick up
Lu from school without first asking
Mama or Papa for permission:

Mama, Papa, Phil, Grandma, Grandpa,
Aunt Julia, Mrs. Baker, Annie
(but only to the playground behind
the house)

Lu does not go with <u>anyone</u> else.

She'll only go with someone else
if Mama or Papa has told her to
beforehand.

Lu has to wait today after school.
Almost all the other children have already been picked up.
Only Lu is standing alone outside.

A woman comes by. "Hello, Lu!" she says. "What are you doing here alone? Come on, I'll take you with me. We're headed the exact same way."

"I don't know you, so I won't go with you!" Lu says.

"But Lu, we know each other," the woman says.

Of course, Lu knows she is Ms. Smith. She lives in the same neighborhood as Lu.

But what is her first name?

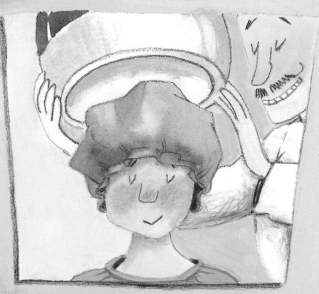

Does she dye her hair red, or is that its natural color?

Does Ms. Smith prefer taking a shower or a bath?

And what's the name of her little dog?

Lu does not know any of that.

"I don't know you, so I won't go with you!" Lu says.
"And besides, Mama said I should wait."

Now it's starting to drizzle.

"Come on, Lu!" a man shouts. "I'm just on the way to your house now."

"I don't know you, so I won't go with you," Lu says.

"Now, wait a minute!" The man laughs. "Don't you know my name?"

Lu does know that. The man is named Ralph. And he's helping Papa build a bicycle shed in their yard.

But what is Ralph's last name?

Does he wash his own stinky socks?

Does he have any pets? Maybe a snake, or a raccoon?

Does he prefer red or green Jell-o?

No idea, Lu thinks.

"I don't know you, so I won't go with you," she says kindly. **"And besides, Mama said I should wait."**

"Well then, see you soon!" Ralph says.

"See you soon!" Lu responds.

A man pulls up in his car.

"Get in quickly—you're getting all wet!" he cries.

"I don't know you, so I won't go with you," Lu says.

"But I know your mom," the man says.
"Now come on!"

"No thank you!" Lu says.

"You're such a stubborn little girl," the man says. "Your mama will be upset with me if I leave you here in the rain!"

"I don't know you, so I won't go with you," Lu says again.

Now the man is offended. He slams the car door and speeds away.

"He's just as stubborn," Lu murmurs. She really doesn't know him. She's only seen the man a few times from a distance.

She does not even know his name.

Or what he likes for breakfast.

Maybe he has a crocodile under his couch at home.

Or does he secretly pick his nose?

No idea, Lu thinks.
And besides, Mama said I should wait.

"Come on, Lu!" a woman calls. "I'll take you under my umbrella!"

"I don't know you, so I won't go with you!" Lu calls, and then laughs. Because that's Mrs. Moser, and Lu actually knows her really well.

Mrs. Moser has a small cat. He's named Rascal.

She lives only two houses away from Lu.

And her favorite food is buttered bread with fresh chives.

But Lu doesn't know if Mrs. Moser exercises in the mornings.

Or whether she snores while she's sleeping.

"Mama said I should wait!"
Lu smiles and winks at Mrs. Moser.

She winks back. "All right," she says. "Maybe another time."

"Yes, maybe," Lu answers.

Someone else appears.

"Come on now, Lu!" he says.

And Lu goes with him.

Because Lu really knows him. This is her brother Phil.

She knows he is afraid of spiders.

His favorite food is vanilla pudding with raspberry sauce.

He still always sleeps with his teddy bear, Gus. No one else knows that, other than Lu.

And he dyes his hair blond himself.

Lu can definitely go with him. And besides, Mama said she should wait for him.

"You're late!" Lu says. "You took so long, I'm practically an old lady by now."

"I'm sorry, Lulabean!" Phil answers. "But now let's hurry. I'm starving!"

"Me too!" Lu says.

You can fill out your own list with your parents or guardians, just as Lu did with her parents.

_____'s List:

People who are allowed to pick up _____ from _____, without first asking _____ for permission:

_____does not go with anyone else.

_____ will only go with someone else if _____has told _____ to beforehand.

Resources for Adults:

International Center for Assault Prevention (ICAP)
Wolverton Center Library
200 College Drive
Blackwood, NJ 08012
Phone: 856-227-7200 ext.4822
Email: childassaultprevention@gmail.com
Website: www.internationalcap.org

National Center for Missing & Exploited Children
Charles B. Wang International Children's Building
699 Prince Street
Alexandria, Virginia 22314-3175
24-hour call center: 1-800-THE-LOST (1-800-843-5678)
Phone: 703-224-2150
Website: www.missingkids.com

The National Crime Prevention Council (NCPC)
2614 Chapel Lake Drive, Suite B
Gambrills, MD 21054
Phone: 443-292-4565
Website: www.ncpc.org

Kidpower
Phone: 800-467-6997
Email: safety@kidpower.org
Website: www.kidpower.org

National Criminal Justice Reference Services (NCJRS)
For resources and publications related to personal safety for children
Website: www.ncjrs.gov/html/ojjdp/psc_english_02/intro.html

Lu's list:

People who are allowed to pick up Lu from school without first asking Mama or Papa for permission:

Mama, Papa, Phil, Grandma, Grandpa, Aunt Julia, Mrs. Baker, Annie (but only to the playground behind the house)

Lu does not go with <u>anyone</u> else.

She'll only go with someone else if Mama or Papa has told her to beforehand.